The Human Condition

The Human Condition
Contemplation and Transformation

Thomas Keating

The Harold M. Wit Lectures
Harvard University
The Divinity School

Introduction by Ronald F. Thiemann

Foreword by Elaine Pagels

PAULIST PRESS
NEW YORK, N.Y. • MAHWAH, N.J.

Cover design and illustration by Emil Antonucci

Copyright © 1999, St. Benedict's Monastery, Snowmass, CO.

Library of Congress Cataloging-in-Publication Data

Keating, Thomas.
    The human condition : contemplation and transformation / Thomas Keating ; introduction by Ronald F. Thiemann ; foreword by Elaine Pagels.
      p.   cm. — (The Wit lectures)
    ISBN 0-8091-3882-4
    1. Contemplation. 2. Spiritual life—Psychology. I. Title. II. Series.
BV5091.C7K418 1999
248.3´4—dc21   99–23044
                                                  CIP

Published by Paulist Press
997 Macarthur Boulevard
Mahwah, New Jersey 07430

www.paulistpress.com

Printed and bound in the
United States of America

THE HAROLD M. WIT LECTURES
Published by Paulist Press

Foreword

Father Thomas Keating writes with the simplicity and depth that emerge from more than fifty years of practicing to become a "friend of God"—in his case as a Cistercian monk, abbot, and spiritual advisor.

What many of us especially appreciate about Thomas Keating is the work he has done—and continues to do—to make accessible the practice of Centering Prayer. In this practice, Father Keating has melded elements of Christian mystical tradition into a practice elementary enough for any of us to learn, but which, over time, may help effect a process of spiritual transformation.

Without discriminating in the ways that most Christians do between those we call Catholic, Protestant, Orthodox, agnostic, Jew, Buddhist, or by other designations, Father Keating attempts to reintroduce into the lives of those he teaches insights and practices that Christian tradition sometimes has suppressed and often has left in obscurity. These two talks begin with a question of self-knowledge and end by recalling the unconditional love of God.

In my own life, I cannot imagine having endured certain difficult times without his generous presence and without the practice he teaches. Thomas

Keating is both a "discerner of spirits," gifted with a charism known from the early days of the Christian movement, and a "psychiatrist" in the original sense of the term—"physician of the soul."

Those of us who learn from him are grateful for—and blessed by—his gifts.

Elaine Pagels
Princeton University

Introduction

In 1997, Father Thomas Keating became the fifth person to deliver the Harold M. Wit Lecture on Living a Spiritual Life in the Contemporary Age at Harvard Divinity School.

Born in New York City in 1923, Father Keating entered the Cistercian Order in 1944 in Valley Falls, Rhode Island. Fourteen years later he was appointed superior of St. Benedict's Monastery in Snowmass, Colorado, and in 1961 he was elected abbot of St. Joseph's Abbey, a large Cistercian monastery in Spencer, Massachusetts.

After two decades in Spencer, he returned in 1981 to Snowmass, where he established a program of intensive ten-day retreats in the practice that he calls Centering Prayer, a contemporary form of the Christian contemplative tradition.

Father Keating is one of the architects of the Centering Prayer movement and of Contemplative Outreach, a support system for those on the contemplative path. He is also a former chairman of Monastic Interreligious Dialogue, which sponsors exchanges between monks and nuns of the world's religions; a member of the International Committee for Peace Council, which fosters dialogue and cooperation among the world's religions; and a member of the Snowmass Interreligious Conference, a group of teachers from the world's religions who meet yearly to share their experience of the spiritual journey in their respective traditions.

He is the author of several best-selling books on the contemplative tradition, including *Open Mind Open Heart, The Mystery of Christ, Invitation to Love,* and *Intimacy with God.*

When he visited Harvard Divinity School, Father Keating delivered two lectures and led a service of Centering Prayer in the chapel of Andover Hall. In an era when the commodification of spirituality in America seems inescapable, his presence and message were genuinely inspiring and encouraging. Thus he fulfilled the desire of Harold M. Wit, who established the lecture series in 1988, to bring to Harvard "unusual individuals who radiate in their thought, word, and being those spiritual qualities and values that have been so inspiring and encouraging to me along my path."

The publication of these lectures gives me the chance once again to acknowledge with gratitude Harold Wit, a generous benefactor of Harvard Divinity School, and to thank Thomas Keating for bringing together in these lectures the Christian contemplative tradition with insights from contemporary psychology. May his lectures serve as a guide to "true peace, sane counsel, and spiritual comfort in God," in the words of *The Cloud of Unknowing*, the fourteenth-century English spiritual classic on which Centering Prayer is largely based.

Ronald F. Thiemann
Harvard Divinity School
Cambridge, Massachusetts

The Human Condition

Where are you? This is one of the great questions of all time. It is the focus of the first half of the spiritual journey.

Biblical scholars and readers will remember that in Genesis 3 it is the question God asked when Adam and Eve had taken off for the underbrush after their disobedience. He called out to them and said, "Adam, where are you?" They were hiding in the woods, and God was looking for them. Adam said, "We heard your voice, and we were scared because we were naked." So God said, "How did you know you were naked?"

This marvelous story of creation is not just about Adam and Eve. It is really about us. It is a revelation of where *we* are. The same question is addressed to every generation, time, and person. At every moment of our lives, God is asking us, "*Where* are you? Why are you hiding?"

All the questions that are fundamental to human happiness arise when we ask ourselves this excruciating question: *Where* am I? Where am I in relation to God, to myself, and to others? These are the basic questions of human life.

As soon as we answer honestly, we have begun the spiritual search for God, which is also the search for ourselves. God is asking us to face the reality of the human condition, to come out of the woods into the full light of intimacy with him. That is the state of mind that Adam and Eve had, according to the story, before their disobedience. As soon as they became aware of their separation from God, they headed for the woods. They had to hide from God because the loss of the intimacy and union that they had enjoyed with him in paradise was so painful.

Sometimes it helps to turn to a story from another spiritual tradition; in juxtaposing the two stories, we may get a new insight. Here is a Sufi tale that is also about the human condition.

A Sufi master had lost the key to his house and was looking for it in the grass outside. He got down on his hands and knees and started running his fingers through every blade of grass. Along came eight or ten of his disciples. They said, "Master, what is wrong?"

He said, "I have lost the key to my house."

They said, "Can we help you find it?"

He said, "I'd be delighted."

So they all got down on their hands and knees

and started running their fingers through the grass.

As the sun grew hotter, one of the more intelligent disciples said, "Master, have you any idea where you might have lost the key?"

The Master replied, "Of course. I lost it in the house."

To which they all exclaimed, "Then why are we looking for it out here?"

He said, "Isn't it obvious? There is more light here."

We have all lost the key to our house. We don't live there anymore. We don't experience the divine indwelling. We don't live with the kind of intimacy with God that Adam and Eve reportedly enjoyed in the Garden of Eden and the Sufi master seems to have enjoyed before he lost his key.

The house in the parable represents happiness, and happiness is intimacy with God, the experience of God's loving presence. Without that experience, nothing else quite works; with it, almost anything works.

This is the human condition—to be without the true source of happiness, which is the experience of the presence of God, and to have lost the key to happiness, which is the contemplative dimension of life, the path to the increasing assimilation and enjoyment of God's presence. What we experience is our desperate search for happiness where it cannot possibly be found. The key is not in the grass; it was not lost outside ourselves. It was lost inside ourselves. That is where we need to look for it.

The chief characteristic of the human condition is that everybody is looking for this key and nobody knows where to find it. The human condition is thus poignant in the extreme. If you want help as you look for the key in the wrong place, you can get plenty of it, because everybody is looking for it in the wrong place, too: where there is more light, pleasure, security, power, acceptance by others. We have a sense of solidarity in the search without any possibility of finding what we are looking for.

Metaphysics and the religions of the world have discovered the insight that human beings are designed for unlimited happiness, the enjoyment of all truth, and love without end. This spiritual hunger is part of our nature as beings with a spiritual dimension. Here we are, with an unbounded desire for happiness and not the slightest idea of where to look for it.

In Roman Catholic theology, original sin is an explanation for why Adam and Eve lost the intimacy they had enjoyed with God. God used to visit them in the cool of the evening. They had an easy relationship with him. As soon as they fell into a discriminating mind by eating of the tree of the knowledge of good and evil, they became self-conscious; they experienced themselves not only as separate from God but also, because of their sin, as alienated from God.

Contemporary psychology has a significant contribution to make at this point. Infants do not have self-consciousness, or at least they have a very small amount. It emerges gradually through various stages of a child's development. Full self-reflective consciousness begins around the ages of twelve to fourteen. Prior to that time, we have an innate thirst for happiness but no practical experience of the presence of the divine within us. So we look for happiness somewhere else.

In the Old Testament, substitutes for the divine presence were called demons or false gods. If we can grasp the fact that only the experience of God can put into perspective all other forms of pleasure or the promises of happiness that various creatures provide, then we will realize that we are looking for happiness in the grass, in the wrong places. All the help we can get from other people who experience the same psychological privation won't do a bit of good.

According to St. Augustine's theology, original sin has three consequences: (1) we don't know where happiness is to be found (ignorance); (2) we look for it in the wrong places (concupiscence); and

(3) if we ever find out where it might be found, the will is too weak to pursue it anyway. That is the somewhat dismal view that Christianity has offered up to now. If you are a Buddhist, you can track the same sort of idea in the teaching about suffering and the cessation of suffering.

Contemporary psychology has provided us with knowledge of the unconscious. The discovery is only a hundred years old, and it casts an enormous light on all spiritual disciplines. In recent years, we have witnessed the development of various psychological theories such as codependency and the dysfunctional family, which assert that more and more people, at least in the Western world, are afflicted by these pathologies (as much as 95 to 98 percent of the population). These theories are getting pretty close to the idea of the universal character of original sin.

But the spiritual journey is more than a psychological process. It is of course primarily a process of grace. God also speaks to us through nature. The more we know about nature, the more we know about the mind of God. Einstein believed that science was directed toward discovering God's thoughts. Quantum physics itself is a kind of spirituality insofar as it is always looking farther into the unknown to see what is beyond the known. It is a search for ultimate reality.

God is available through many sources besides the religious quest. I don't mean to imply that psychology replaces the work of religion, but it seems to me that it greatly supports religion and brings a certain clarity to areas of the human condition, especially the discovery of the unconscious.

All of us have been through the process of being born and entering this world with three essential biological needs: security and survival, power and control, affection and esteem. Without adequate fulfillment of these biological needs, we probably would not survive infancy. Since the experience of the presence of God is not there at the age we start to develop self-consciousness, these three instinctual needs are all we have with which to build a program for happiness. Without the help of reason to modify them, we build a universe with ourselves at the center, around which all our human faculties revolve like planets around the sun. As a result, any object entering into our universe—another person or event—is judged on the basis of whether it can provide us with what we believe or demand happiness to be.

Children who are deprived of security, affection, and control needs develop a desperate drive to find more and more symbols of these basic human needs in their culture. This is called compensation. It can also happen that when experiences in early childhood are unbearable, they are repressed into

13

the unconscious. The body seems to be a kind of warehouse in which all our experiences—the whole of our lives—are recorded. We don't need to have our lives recorded by the angels anymore, because we know that there is a neurological process that takes care of that for us. Some who have had near-death experiences report that they experienced reruns of their whole lives.

Here, then, is the beginning of what might be called the addictive process, the need to hide the pain that we suffered in early life and cannot face. We repress it into the unconscious to provide an apparent freedom from the pain or develop compensatory processes to access forms of pleasure that offset the pain we are not yet prepared to face. We are thrust because of circumstances into the position of developing a homemade self that does not conform to reality. Everything entering into the world that makes survival and security, affection and esteem, and power and control our chief pursuits of happiness has to be judged on the basis of one question: Is it good for *me*? Hence, good and evil are judged not by their objective reality, but by the way we perceive them as fitting into our private universe or not.

At age four or five, the situation gets more complicated. As we begin to socialize, we internalize the values of family, peer group, religion, ethnic group, nationality, race, gender, and sexual orientation. The combination of these two forces—the drive for happiness in the form of security and survival, affection and esteem, and power and control, and overidentification with the particular group to which we belong—greatly complicates our emotional programs for happiness. In our younger days, this development is normal. As adults, activity arising from such motivation is childish.

The homemade self or the false self, as it is usually called, is programmed for human misery. Temperament of course also plays a part. Our emotional programs are filtered through our temperamental biases, number on the Eneagram, or identification with a particular archetype. If we have an aggressive temperament and like to dominate as many events and people as possible, that drive increases in proportion to the felt privations of that need that we suffered in early childhood. Without facing these early childhood excesses and trying to dismantle or moderate them through the exercise of reason (in Christian tradition this means the practice of virtue), they continue to exert enormous influence throughout life. For example, people who want power always want to dictate what is going to happen in every situation. They cannot be happy unless they do. As soon as they are frustrated, off go the afflictive emotions: grief, despair, and anger. There is nothing wrong with these instinctual needs. But because there was no experience of God at the age that would have moderated their excessive importance, such individuals mistakenly sink all of their hope of finding happiness into the pursuit of one or all of these needs.

As soon as we notice we are annoyed or angry about something, we tend to protect ourselves by projecting the cause of our upsetting emotion onto a situation or another person: "They" did this to me. "They" are always a problem. But, in fact, the real problem is not "them" but us. All biases and prejudices are the attitudes of a child from ages four to eight. If they are present in us, we are still functioning at the level of a preadolescent.

Our innocence as children is the innocence of ignorance. Consciousness in the first stages of human life is very limited. The infant is at one with everything that is happening until that unity is lost somewhere between the ages of two and three. When thinking and self-reflection begin, since the experience of God is missing, some other form of happiness has to take its place, just for the sake of survival.

The distortion of human nature becomes habitual and is supported, like the Sufi master's disciples, by others who are doing the same thing—trying to find happiness where it cannot possibly be found.

When Jesus said, "Repent," to his first disciples, he was calling them to change the direction in which they were looking for happiness. "Repent" is an invitation to grow up and become a fully mature human being who integrates the biological needs with the rational level of consciousness. The rational level of consciousness is the door that swings into higher states—the intuitive and unitive levels of consciousness. They open us to the experience of God's presence, which restores the sense of happiness. We can then take possession of everything that was good in our early life while leaving the distortions behind.

The false self is deeply entrenched. You can change your name and address, religion, country, and clothes. But as long as you don't ask *it* to change, the false self simply adjusts to the new environment. For example, instead of drinking your friends under the table as a significant sign of self-worth and esteem, if you enter a monastery, as I did, *fasting* the other monks under the table could become your new path to glory. In that case, what would have changed? Nothing.

We can be converted to the values of the Gospel of Jesus Christ and do the best we can to moderate the excesses of our desperate search for security, affection and esteem, and power and control, while our basic attitudes remain the same. This is how conversion is distinguished from external changes of lifestyle. Conversion addresses the heart of the problem. Jesus has some harsh sayings that are incomprehensible unless we see them in the light of the harm that our emotional programs are doing. For example, Jesus said, "If your foot scandalizes you, cut it off." He wasn't recommending self-mutilation but was saying that if your emotional programs are so close to you that you love them as much as your own hand or foot or eye, get rid of them. They are programs for human misery that will never work. They will interfere with all your relationships—with God, yourself, other people, the earth, and the cosmos.

When we are converted to a new way of life, to service or to a particular ministry, we often experience a wonderful gift of freedom and a radical change of direction. Perhaps you have made enormous sacrifices in your business or profession, maybe even in family life, to be able to begin a journey into the service of the Gospel. But watch out! All the emotional programs for happiness, overidentification with one's group, and the commentaries that reinforce our innate tendencies have sources in the unconscious as well as in the conscious.

That is why St. Paul could say, "What I want to do, I don't do. And what I don't want to do I find myself doing" (Rom 7:15ff.). If we don't face the consequences of unconscious motivation—through a practice or discipline that opens us to the unconscious—then that motivation will secretly influence our decisions all through our lives.

One needs a willingness to be exposed to the unconscious. This requires some courage and persistence. We can't call up the unconscious at will. With the help of psychotherapy, we might be able to call up some of it. The dark nights described by St. John of the Cross go much deeper. Normally, emotions need to be expressed in some way in order to be processed. Emotions are energy. If they are not processed, they become blocks in our bodies and nervous systems to the free flow of our energy systems and of grace.

When we are not thinking, analyzing, or planning and place ourselves in the presence of God in faith, we open ourselves to the contents of the unconscious. We should do this gradually so as not to be overtaken by an overwhelming explosion of emotion. A generation ago, in the psychedelic era, people opened themselves to the unconscious before they had the humility or the devotion to God to be able to handle it. The unconscious needs to be respected and approached with prudence.

Someone who is involved in a contemplative prayer practice needs guidance. It may not be available in every spiritual guide who comes along.

What matters most is fidelity to the daily practice of a contemplative form of prayer such as Centering Prayer. This gradually exposes us to the unconscious at a rate that we can handle and places us under the guidance of the Holy Spirit. Divine love then prepares us to receive the maximum that God can possibly communicate of his inner light. Besides the dark side of the unconscious, there are all kinds of other awesome energies—for example, natural talents, the fruits of the Spirit, the seven gifts of the Spirit, and the divine indwelling itself—that we haven't experienced yet and that are waiting to be discovered.

It is never too late to start the spiritual journey or to start over, and it is worth starting over any number of times. If you are over eighty, you will be happy to know that there is an accelerated course. I wouldn't be surprised if, in the course of dying, there are all kinds of transforming experiences. What God is after are our good intention and our efforts. We may not experience the fruit of our efforts in this life, but just keep trying.

The contemplative journey, because it involves the purification of the unconscious, is not a magic carpet to bliss. It is an exercise of letting go of the false self, a humbling process, because it is the only self we know.

God approaches us from many different perspectives: illness, misfortune, bankruptcy, divorce proceedings, rejection, inner trials. God has not promised to take away our trials, but to help us to change our attitudes toward them. That is what holiness really is. In this life, happiness is rooted in our basic attitude toward reality.

Sometimes a sense of failure is a great means to true humility, which is what God most looks for in us. I realize this is not the language of success, but we have oversubscribed to that language. We need to hear about the interior freedom that comes through participation in the sufferings of Christ, the symbol of God's love for everyone on earth.

In the coming millennium, religious leaders and spiritual teachers might consider as their primary responsibility not so much to convert new constituents or new followers to a particular form of meditation, but to create communion—harmony, understanding, and respect for everyone in the human family, especially the members of other religions.

In the world that lies ahead, religious pluralism is going to penetrate all cultures. How we live together with different points of view is going to become more and more important. I don't know whether we can make progress in such a project without a contemplative practice that alerts us to our own biases, prejudices, and self-centered programs for happiness, especially when they trample on other people's rights and needs.

Some people enter religious life looking for the family they never had. But religious life isn't that kind of family. Some people get married because they want the mother who did the laundry and provided a shoulder to cry on. Many people who enter marriage are too immature to handle its responsibilities. That is why they often break up and have to start over. But if they are not aware of the unconscious factors that caused the breakdown of the first marriage, they will just bring the same problems into the next marriage.

The false self is looking for fame, power, wealth, and prestige. The unconscious is very powerful until the divine light of the Holy Spirit penetrates to its depths and reveals its dynamics. Here is where the great teaching of the dark nights of St. John of the Cross corresponds to depth psychology, only the work of the Holy Spirit goes far deeper. Instead of trying to free us from what interferes with our ordinary human life, the Spirit calls us to transformation of our inmost being, and indeed of all our faculties, into the divine way of being and acting.

The Greek Fathers called this process *deification*. God has called us through the Gospel into an adventure in faith, hope, and love that involves being introduced to the inner life of the Ultimate Reality, whom we call God in the Christian tradition. The same unconditional love that moves in God is moving in us by grace, supplanting the human ego with the divine "I." We begin to manifest in daily life not our false selves and prejudices, but the infinite tenderness of God, the concern of God for every living thing, especially for the needy and the poor.

Without profound purification, how far can social action actually extend? People involved in social action have a false self, too. They need to know the dynamics that are at work within them. Otherwise, social projects may fall apart, or they will suffer burnout.

"*Where* are you?" is, indeed, a question of great magnitude. Are you still at the age of one or two, where your emotional program for security is the chief energy that determines your decisions and relationships, especially the relationship between God and you? Are you so enamored with your religion that you have a naive loyalty that cannot see the real faults that are present in a particular faith community? Do you sweep under the rug embarrassing situations and bow to the security or esteem needs of the community?

All human history is under the influence of the false-self system that easily moves from our hearts into our families, communities, and nations and then afflicts the whole human race. God invites us to take responsibility for being human and to open ourselves to the unconscious damage that is influencing our decisions and relationships.

If psychologists and psychiatrists would be in dialogue with the insights of St. John of the Cross and those who experience the dark nights, there could be a marvelous symbiosis of treatment. We are not sick just because of some physiological pathology. It is not just a question of sin either; it is a question of the human condition, for which none of us is initially responsible but, on becoming adults, we are now called to be responsible.

How do we cultivate any friendship? By spending time together with those to whom we are attracted. There are stages of building any relationship, beginning with getting acquainted, which is a bit awkward; through friendliness, which is more pleasant; to friendship, which is a commitment; to various levels of union and unity that restore the state of intimacy that was lost symbolically in the Garden of Eden.

Here we are under the influence of unconscious drives of various intensity that in turn influence our decisions and relationships with other people and foul them up. We have to begin to take the trail to truth. This is what the Gospel invites us to do.

We don't know much about the prayer life of

Jesus. St. Paul urged his disciples to pray without ceasing. Contemplative prayer is a deepening of faith that moves beyond thoughts and concepts. One just listens to God, open and receptive to the divine presence in one's inmost being as its source. One listens not with a view to hearing something, but with a view to becoming aware of the obstacles to one's friendship with God.

Contemplative prayer starts modestly, but as soon as it begins to reach a certain intensity, it opens us to the unconscious. Painful memories that we have forgotten or repressed begin to come to consciousness. Primitive emotions that we felt as children and that we have been compensating for may come to consciousness.

How should we handle these afflictive emotions? By facing them, by feeling them. Feelings that have been repressed have to be allowed to pass through our awareness once again in order to be left behind for good. Most of the time, they don't need psychotherapy; they just need to be evacuated. We might say that we are suffering from acute psychic indigestion, a nausea of a psychological character that is interfering with our mental health and all our relationships.

In contemplative prayer, the rest we experience is so deep that it allows the inner defenses to relax, and the body, with its great capacity for health, says, "Let's get rid of these emotional blocks once and for all." The psychic nervous system may explode in primitive emotions or intolerable memories. For a few minutes, you feel that you would rather be in hell. But then it is over.

Some problems, admittedly, are so serious that one needs psychiatric help. It is important that there be teamwork between spiritual guides and psychological professionals. If we are talking about the health of a human being, we are not just talking about the body or even the emotions; we are talking about the whole range of human potential, including spiritual health. These all have to be treated at once if we want to get well. This is what contemplative prayer does. But it doesn't act alone. Its fruits need to be worked into daily life.

Contemplative prayer begins to make us aware of the divine presence within us, the source of true happiness. As soon as we begin to taste the peace that comes from the regular practice of contemplative prayer, it relativizes the whole unreal world of demands and "shoulds," of aversions and desires that were based on emotional programs for happiness that might have worked for children, but that are, in fact, killing us.

"*Where* are you?" God's question to us never changes. In some cases, life has been so tragic that we are not free to decide where we are. But the power of divine grace, especially as it is experienced in contemplative prayer, opens us to the unconscious and introduces us to a world of unlimited possibilities that are unknown to us now.

Every human pleasure is meant to be a stepping-stone to knowing God better or to discovering some new aspect of God. Only when that stepping-stone becomes an end in itself—that is, when we overidentify with it—does it distort the divine intention. Everything in the universe is meant to be a reminder of God's presence.

God is existence. In everything that exists, God is present. The greatest reality is God's presence. The problem is that we only access that presence to the degree that our interior life is attuned to it. Hence the importance in the Christian tradition of listening to sacred scripture, which is much more than just listening to its literal meaning. It is sitting with the text in the presence of the Holy Spirit and allowing the Spirit to deepen our capacity to listen. That in no way denigrates the value of the literal; listening simply doesn't stop there. The external word of God is designed to awaken the presence of the word of God in us. When that happens, we become, in a certain sense, the word of God.

The presence of God begins to be felt very gently. As it becomes stronger and more pervasive, it initiates a gradual return to the state of intimacy that the story of the Garden of Eden describes in mythological form. (Mythology is not untruth; it is simply an attempt to speak the truth in a symbolic way that points to a reality beyond words or concepts.)

The Gospel introduces us to the divine therapy for the illness of the human condition in the form of contemplative prayer, which addresses not only the distortions of our conscious behavior, but also the dynamics of the unconscious. Contemplation provides us with the courage to face the second great question of the spiritual journey: *Who* are you?

Contemplation and the Divine Therapy

Who are you? That is the great question of the second half of the spiritual journey.

All of us come into this world as little bundles of emotional needs, of which we can identify three in particular: security and survival, affection and esteem, and power and control.

Without these needs being met in some degree, infants would withdraw in depression and apathy and eventually die from psychological starvation. Hence the significance of these basic human needs and the extraordinary effect that the providing or withholding, real or imaginary, of these biological needs has on the rest of our lives.

The energy that we put into trying to find happiness in fulfilling these emotional needs tends to increase with time. The painful sense of early rejection may be repressed into the unconscious, where it continues to affect how we react to daily life and our adult decisions. Our experience of life on the ordinary psychological level is normally one of being dominated by external events and our emotional reactions to them. Some of this is conscious, but much of it is rooted in the unconscious. This is the illness of the human condition from which we all suffer.

Daily life constantly triggers events that frustrate our emotional programs for happiness. Then such afflictive emotions as fear, anger, and discouragement arise automatically. The fact that we experience anxiety and annoyance is the certain sign that, in the unconscious, there is an emotional program for happiness that has just been frustrated.

Human nature is so designed that our imagination and emotions work together, like the interaction of the wheels of an old clock. As soon as we start to be upset by any emotion, the imagination immediately responds by calling up the prerecorded tapes that are appropriate to the level of intensity of the emotion.

This is happening to us every day to some degree, from the fairly mild to the very extreme. Our unconscious value systems are often challenged by some particular event or person. Immediately we are in the midst of an intense interior dialogue as well as emotional turmoil. If we don't reverse the process, then every time that cycle occurs, we are "reincarnated" in the same old emotional programs for happiness and their inevitable frustrations. Is this the way to lead a human life? It is into this situation that Jesus arrives on the scene with his exhortation to repent, to change our conscious and unconscious motivations; to change, in short, where we are looking for happiness. We need the divine therapy.[1]

The divine therapy, like Alcoholics Anonymous, is based on the realization that you know where you are and that your life is unmanageable. We may be able to lead a relatively normal life, but there is no experience of the true happiness that comes from letting go of the obstacles to the awareness of the divine presence.

Spiritual awareness is designed by God to become our normal awareness. To what might we liken our awareness in ordinary daily life? It is like being at a good movie where we identify with the characters on the screen. We may even forget that we are in the movie house. In similar fashion, unless our selfish programs for happiness have begun to be dismantled by a spiritual practice or discipline, we are not aware that events and people or our plans and memories are dominating our awareness from morning to night.

Suppose that through a practice like Centering Prayer, which prepares us for contemplation, the primary locus of the divine therapy, we take half an hour every day for solitude and silence, just to be with God and with ourselves (without knowing yet who that is). As a result of the deep rest and silence

---

1. For a fuller discussion of the divine therapy, see Thomas Keating, *Intimacy with God* (New York: Continuum Publishing Co., 1996).

that come through such a practice, our emotional programs begin to be relativized. They were designed at a time when we didn't know the goodness and the reassurance of God's presence.

The presence of God is true security. There really isn't any other. Divine love is the full affirmation of who we are. Interior freedom is the gift of God as we let go of our attachments and aversions, our "shoulds," and the emotional programs of happiness that we bring with us from early childhood and that are totally impracticable in adult life.

Through a spiritual practice like Centering Prayer, we begin to experience spiritual awareness. Ordinary life then becomes like a lousy movie where we don't identify with the characters or plot. We can get up and leave—something we can't do in daily life when we overidentify with our ordinary stream of awareness and its contents. That is the inner tyranny that opposes true freedom. The freedom of the children of God means we can *decide* what to do about particular events. We live more and more out of self-actuating motivation rather than the domination of our habitual drives to be esteemed, to be in control, to feel secure.

Centering Prayer and other practices that lead to Christian contemplation move us toward interior freedom. We open ourselves to God and allow ourselves to rest in a silent place beyond thinking, a kind of oasis in a day of emotional turmoil. Even from a purely human perspective, everybody needs some solitude and silence in daily life, just to be human and creative about the way one lives.

This sort of spiritual discipline is a therapy for the tyranny of the false self, not only for our emotional programs for happiness, but also for our overidentification with family, nation, religion, or group. Of course we owe a measure of gratitude to our nation, religion, and family. But it is interesting that Jesus said that unless we hate our parents, we can't be his disciples. By this he didn't mean that we should not love and respect them and care for them in their old age, as commanded by the Fourth Commandment of the Torah, but that we should not have a naive loyalty to a particular group (even one's family) that disregards injustices that need to be corrected. Sometimes, for the sake of peace or in order to be loved, one sweeps serious problems under the rug instead of dealing with them in honesty and truth.

Once a regular practice of Centering Prayer has been established, we move normally in each period of prayer toward a place of rest where our faculties are relatively calm and quiet. Thoughts are coming downstream, but as we learn to disregard them, we begin to enjoy a sense of the divine presence. Beyond our thinking and emotional experience is the deeper reality of the spiritual level of our being. It is another way of knowing reality that is unlike ordinary psychological awareness. As a result, not only is the mind quiet and at rest from the ordinary concerns of daily life, but the body also begins to rest, a rest that is deeper than sleep.

Repressed material in the unconscious is vigorously defended by our various inclinations and biases, especially by our emotional investment in particular programs for happiness rooted in the unconscious. The deep rest of Centering Prayer loosens up the defense mechanisms that have kept an emotional trauma in early childhood from confronting us. One of the most devastating emotional traumas of early childhood is physical or sexual abuse. The damage done to the delicate emotional lives of children is so painful that it is repressed into the unconscious, where it may remain unknown by the victim unless deep psychotherapy or contemplative prayer loosens up the defense mechanisms.

Centering Prayer is not an end in itself, but its deep rest loosens up the emotional weeds of a lifetime. When our defenses go down, up comes the dark side of the personality, the dynamics of the unconscious, and the immense emotional investment we have placed in false programs for happiness, along with the realization of how immersed we are in our particular cultural conditioning.

Everybody is culturally conditioned to some degree. Even the greatest saints only reach a certain degree of freedom from cultural overidentification. That overidentification is challenged in Centering Prayer. We spend the first part of our lives finding a role—becoming a mother or father, a professor, a doctor, a minister, a soldier, a business person, an artisan, or whatever. The paradox is that we can never fully fulfill our role until we are ready to let it go. Whoever we think we are, we are not. We have to find that out, and the best way to do so, or at least the most painless way, is through the process that we call the spiritual journey. This requires facing the dark side of our personality and the emotional investment we have made in false programs for happiness and in our particular cultural conditioning.

Rest in Centering Prayer provides us with profound healing. To be really healed requires that we allow our dark side to come to full consciousness and then to let it go and give it to God. The divine therapy is an agreement that we make with God. We recognize that our own ideas of happiness are not going to work, and we turn our lives over completely to God.

What happens during this process is a certain unloading of primitive emotions or a bombardment of thoughts that we never expected to have on the spiritual journey. To evacuate that material, all we have to do, under normal circumstances, is to wave good-bye as it passes through our awareness. Then, when we return to our original intention—usually through some symbol of turning inwardly to God, such as saying a sacred word or following the breath as a sacred experience—this process starts over again. We move toward rest. The rest, when deep, releases repressed material from the unconscious. We experience a kind of psychic nausea and then a sense of freedom from having gotten rid of a wad of undigested psychological data from early childhood. To submit to the divine therapy is something we owe to ourselves and the rest of humanity. If we don't allow the Spirit of God to address the deep levels of our attachments to ourselves and to our programs for happiness, we will pour into the world the negative elements of our self-centeredness, adding to the conflicts and social disasters that come from overidentifying with the biases and prejudices of our particular culture and upbringing. This is becoming more important as we move into a global culture and into the increasing pluralism of religious beliefs.

What are we going to do when we are surrounded with people whose belief systems are quite different from our own? Where will our support come from? Instead of finding support that will back up our own belief system, we might look more profitably for the self-differentiation that enables us to be fully ourselves, with the acceptance of our limitations. As we become more aware of the dynamics of our unconscious, we can receive people and events as they are, rather than filtered through what we would like them to be, expect them to be, or demand them to be. This requires letting go of the attachments, aversions, "shoulds," and demands on others and on life that reflect the mentality of a child rather than that of a grownup. The latter, under normal conditions, is responsible for his or her choices.

This is a big project, but it is not yet spiritual maturity. It is just human growth into full, responsible, self-reflective consciousness. It is the first step that the Gospel invites us to take in the process of repentance. Daily life, if one is alert to the dynamics of the unconscious, brings us to new levels of realization not only about *where* we are but *who* we are.

None of us knows until we have been through difficult problems and tragedies what we would do in a challenging situation. Once I attended a panel discussion of people who had suffered during the Holocaust and other barbaric oppressions of this century. One woman on the panel had survived the Holocaust, but her parents had been killed. She had started a humanitarian organization to prevent such horrors from being repeated and mentioned casually, "You know, I couldn't have started that organization unless I knew that, with the situation just a little different, I could have done the same things that the Nazis did to my parents and the others in the concentrations camps."

This woman, it seems to me, possessed true humility—the knowledge of one's self that clearly perceives that with just a little change of circumstances, one is capable of any evil.

The spiritual journey is not a career or a success story. It is a series of humiliations of the false self that become more and more profound. These make room inside us for the Holy Spirit to come in and heal. What prevents us from being available to God is gradually evacuated. We keep getting closer and closer to our center. Every now and then God lifts a corner of the veil and enters into our awareness through various channels, as if to say, "Here I am. Where are you? Come and join me."

In the Near East, centuries ago successive cultures built new cities on top of the last ones. For some reason, people didn't bother using new space; they just burned down what was there when they defeated an enemy and built something new. The ruins of these ancient cities built one on top of the other are called "tells." The spiritual journey is like an archaeological dig through the various stages of our lives, from where we are now back through the midlife crisis, adult life, adolescence, puberty, early childhood, infancy. What happens if we allow that archaeological dig to continue? We feel that we are getting worse. But we are really not getting worse; we are just finding out how bad off we always were. That is an enormous grace.

From a vertical point of view, our conversion begins at the place we are now in our relationship to God. First we clear off the brush, stones, and debris at the top of our interior "tell." Our agreement with the divine therapist is to allow the Holy Spirit to bring us to the truth about ourselves. This initial period of conversion corresponds to the springtime of the spiritual life, when prayer is easy, and we have great energy in pursuing practices of self-denial, various forms of prayer, ministry, and other forms of social service. As we begin to trust God more, we enjoy a certain freedom from our vices and may often experience great satisfaction in our spiritual endeavors.

When God decides we are ready, he invites us to a new level of self-knowledge. God withdraws the initial consolations of conversion, and we are plunged in darkness, spiritual dryness, and confusion. We think that God has abandoned us. Because we don't enjoy the same emotional experiences as before, we think that God must have departed for the next universe and couldn't care less about us. This is especially poignant for people who have felt rejection in early life; now they feel they have been rejected by God, and that is the ultimate rejection. The dark nights are especially tough on them. But if they can wait them out, they will be completely healed of their sense of rejection for good when they rediscover God at a deeper level of faith.

Instead of going away, God simply moves downstairs, so to speak, and waits for us to come and join him. Perhaps God wonders what the grumbling is all about.

What makes us think God has gone away? The divine presence can't go away. God is existence and fills everything that exists (St. Thomas Aquinas). The Gospel teaches that Christ is present *in* the storm, not just emerging from the storm.

Some films are like the parables in the Gospel; they bring to our attention moral, social, and spiritual issues that we wouldn't otherwise learn about through the medium of ordinary words. I remember seeing the movie *Love Story* and for three days afterward, I was in tears. The plot is simple enough. It concerns a young man and woman who are totally in love with one another, live for each other, and are everything to each other. Then she is diagnosed with an inoperable cancer and in a few months is dead. The whole meaning of his life is wiped out.

In the last scene, we see the man after leaving the hospital where his wife died, walking slowly into the fog, which gets thicker and thicker. He sits down on a park bench. As the movie's theme song plays in the background, the screen just gets darker and darker.

I realized that this was a parable of my experience after putting everything into seeking God and finding more and more delight in the embrace of God's presence in contemplative prayer. Then God seemed to walk out of my life, abandoning me in a church pew, so to speak. In the dark nights, consolations on the spiritual journey, including the rituals and practices that previously supported our faith and devotion, fail us. Faith becomes simply belief in God's goodness without any taste of it. It is trusting in God without knowing whom we are trusting, because the relationship we thought we had with God has disappeared.

Here the great wisdom saying of Jesus comes to mind: "He who seeks only himself brings himself to ruin, whereas he who brings himself to nothing for my sake discovers who he is" (Mt 10:38). To bring oneself to nothing—no thing—is to cease to identify with the tyranny of our emotional programs for happiness and the limitations of our cultural conditioning. They are so strong in our culture that even our language reflects them. We say, "I am angry." But *you* are not angry; you just have angry feelings.

You may say, "I am depressed." No, *you* are not depressed; you have feelings of depression.

It is not feelings that are the problem, but what we do with them that matters. The freedom to deal with them and to confront them with reason and faith is what makes us fully human.

The beginning of our spiritual conversion is followed by a transition period that is always dark, confusing, and confining. Then comes a period of peace, enjoyment of a new inner freedom, the wonder of new insights. That takes time. Rarely is there a sudden movement to a new level of awareness that is permanent.

What happens when we get to the bottom of the pile of our emotional debris? We are in divine union. There is no other obstacle.

As long as we are identified with some role or persona, we are not free to manifest the purity of God's presence. Part of life is a process of dropping whatever role, however worthy, you identify with. It is not you. Your emotions are not you. Your body is not you. If you are not those things, who are you? That is the big question of the second half of the spiritual journey.

The process of spiritual growth is like a spiral staircase. It goes down, and it also goes up. Every movement toward the humiliation of the false self, if we accept it, is a step toward interior freedom and inner resurrection. This new freedom is not control; it is the freedom not to demand of life whatever we used to feel was essential for our particular *idea* of happiness.

The divine therapy is an extraordinary project. Only God could have thought it up, and only God can persuade people to do it. I don't say that this will necessarily happen to everyone. But we are offered the opportunity. The priority we give to the invitation is up to us.

There is an impressive story in the Zen Buddhist tradition, which I presume to paraphrase here, about a meeting of the Buddha toward the end of his life with eighty thousand disciples at a place called Vulture Peak. When they all had gathered there and meditated together for a long time, the Buddha stood on a platform and lifted up a lotus flower with his two hands high above his head. As he did so, all the monks entered into a profound state of oneness with the lotus flower and with all creation.

The silence grew deeper and deeper as they all transcended their personal self-awareness and became lost in the consciousness of the Ultimate Reality. Suddenly, a monk standing next to the Buddha started to laugh. His raucous laughter resounded off the mountaintops and shattered the sacred silence, creating instead in the vast assembly a stunned immobility.

The Buddha slowly lowered the lotus flower and turned to the monk. He immediately handed him the lotus flower, the symbol of imparting to him the fullness of the dharma.

Or, in handing him the lotus flower, did the Buddha simply recognize that this monk, by his laughter, manifested a more sublime state of unity with the Ultimate Reality than all the other monks?

The ultimate abandonment of one's role is not to have a self as a fixed point of reference; it is the freedom to manifest God through one's own uniqueness. This monk had hit bottom. But the bottom in the spiritual journey is also the top. To be no one is to be everyone. To be no self is to be the true Self. To be nothing is to be everything. In a sense, it is to be God. For Christians, it is to be a kind of fifth Gospel: to become the word of God and to manifest God rather than the false self, with its emotional programs for happiness and attachments to various roles, including the most spiritual. When you have been liberated from them all, you are in a space that is both empty of self and full of God.

This monk chose the way of spiritual discipline to become the Other. There is at least one other way of negotiating the spiral staircase. It is by passing through great tragedy or physical and mental suffering. God leads some people through the most terrible anguish and pain to the same place. Here is an example.

A young man with AIDS was dying in a hospital, and he was literally shaking from the fear of death. What had been communicated to him as a child was an emotionally charged idea of God as an implacable judge ready to bring down the verdict of *guilty,* or a harsh policeman ever on the watch—someone you would want to avoid encountering. The young man was afraid of dying and going to meet this hazardous God whom he had heard about in early childhood.

One of the nurses came into his room, and he asked her, "Can you do something to help me?" She said, "I can give you a treatment called therapeutic touch." He replied, "Please do." The nurse began the gentle treatment. At one point his eyes rolled back, and the nurse thought he was going to die, but she kept on with the treatment. When she finished, he opened his eyes and said, "You'll never know what you just did for me. I have experienced unconditional love." About an hour later, he died.

If we have not experienced ourselves as unconditional love, we have more work to do, because that is who we really are.